The Ancestor in Ireland

A Companion Guide

Donal F. Begley

Heraldic Artists Ltd.
Genealogy Bookshop, Nassau Street, Dublin 2, Ireland.

All Rights Reserved. No part of this publication may be reproduced, stored in a retrieval system or transmitted in any form or by any means: electronic, electrostatic, magnetic tape, mechanical, photocopying, recording, or otherwise, without permission in writing from the publishers, Heraldic Artists Ltd.

© Donal F. Begley 1985

I.S.B.N. 0 9502455 8 5

First Impression 1982
Second Impression 1985

Library of Congress Washington
Copyright Certificate
Registration Number
TX 1-015-681

A Publication in The Heraldry and Genealogy Series by
HERALDIC ARTISTS LTD., Nassau Street, Dublin 2.

Printed in Ireland by Mount Salus Press Ltd., Dublin 4.

Contents

Preparing to hit the Ancestor Trail

Exile	5
Homeward Bound	6
Ancestral Stamping Ground	6
Tuning in to the lingo or English as she is spoken in Ireland	6
A Companion Guide	7
Questions Often Asked	7
Getting Started	7
Dublin	7
Birthdates	8
Local Tradition	8
Traditional Recitation of Genealogies	8
The O's and the Mac's	9
Meaning of O-	9
Dropping of O-	9
Meaning of Mac & Mc	9
Surnames — New & Old	10
Christian Name Pattern in the Generations	10
System of Naming the Generations	10
The Naming of the Land	11
Townlands	11
Townland Names: Local Versions	11
Townland Names: Official Versions	11
Parish	12
Barony	12
Barony Names	12
Towns & Villages as Points of Local Reference	12

To the Country in Search of Ancestors

Local Visit	13
Local Institutions	14
Local Library	14
Post Office	14
Baptismal Records	14
Content of Parish Registers	15

Age of Parish Registers	15
Checking Parish Registers	15
Living Relatives	18
Register of Electors	18
County and Local Newspapers	18
Local Publications	19
School Records	19
Headstones	20
Local Assistance	20
Reading Headstone Inscriptions	20
Treatment of Lichen on Headstones	21

Searching the Records: A Checklist

Records of Births, Marriages and Deaths	22
Parish Registers	22
Voters Lists	23
Wills	23
Tithe Listings	23
Rateable Valuation Returns	24
Incumbered Estates Records	24
Owners of Land	25
Registration of Land	25

Seven Wonders of Ireland

New Grange	26
Great Skellig	26
Clonmacnois	26
Bunratty Castle and Folk Park	26
Kilkenny City	27
Trinity College, Dublin	27
Cultra	27

Miscellaneous

County and Branch Libraries	28
County Newspapers and Towns where published	30
Latin forms of Christian Names	30
Area Registries of Births, Marriages and Deaths	31
Useful Books	32
Map of Ireland	16

Preparing to hit the Ancestor Trail

a few facts

Of the numerous men and women who from time beyond recall set sail from the shores of Ireland for distant lands most were destined never again to see their native country. From the sixth century onwards Irish monks and priests began to go forth to a Europe darkened by barbarian hordes in order to rekindle there the flame of Christianity. The exile of those early Irish missionaries was, of course, voluntary and self-imposed, very different from the forced emigration of the last three centuries brought about by war, privation and famine. Beginning about 1650 the outflow of people from Ireland gradually gathered momentum before assuming tidal proportions during the period 1845-1855. That mid 19th century exodus accounts, in the main, for the Irish element in many communities throughout the world today.

Exile

The misery of parting with the homeland and the loneliness of the emigrant in unfamiliar surroundings were given vivid expression in a vast volume of exile music and song. In the very popular *Dear Old Skibbereen,* the author imagines a dialogue between an emigrant father and his son, born in the new world:

'Oh, father dear, I often hear
you speak of Erin's Isle,
Her lofty hills, her mountains grand,
her valleys wild and wide;
They say it is a lovely land
wherein a prince might dwell,
Oh, why did you abandon it,
the reason to me tell.'

'Oh, son, I loved my native land
with energy and pride,
Until a blight came o'er my land,
my sheep and cattle died;
My rent and taxes were too high,
I could not them redeem,
So, that's the why, my reason, boy,
I left old Skibbereen.'

Homeward Bound

Each year sees the return to Ireland of more and more descendants of families who were forced to emigrate, particularly in the 19th century. Some come out of a sense of curiosity, others are impelled by a sense of duty. The Romans had a word for it — *pietas* —, a spirit of faithfulness to the homeland. The ambition of the visitors is to discover the location of their ancestral homestead, to visit the places associated with their ancestors and, if possible, to meet and greet long lost kith and kin.

Ancestral Stamping Ground

On the way to and from the ancestral stamping ground, so to speak, the road may take the visitor past one of the seven glories of ancient and medieval Ireland. A trip to one or more of these marvels described on page 26 should provide a rewarding experience and cap a memorable holiday in Ireland.

Tuning in to the *lingo* or English as she is spoken in Ireland

'Ladies and Gentlemen': we are now approaching the Irish coast. We hope you have enjoyed your flight to Ireland. This is the last time you will hear the King's English until you re-board for your return flight.

'English as she is spoken in Ireland' is an expression of reproof directed by generations of Irish schoolmasters at generations of Irish schoolboys. The visitor is unlikely to be very long in Ireland before he or she senses a certain indirectness of expression in local speech — 'can I ask you if you would have a match' instead of 'have you a match'.

Such roundabout turns of expression so characteristic of everyday speech in Ireland are based on word pattern structures in the Gaelic language. In this situation it is always helpful to know what news topics are on the lips of the people — so one or other of the daily newspapers — *The Irish Times, The Irish Independent, The Irish Press* — is recommended reading.

A Companion Guide

This booklet is in the nature of a companion guide intended for visitors from overseas attempting to explore their family origins in Ireland. It will seek to give them a helping hand in their searches by anticipating many of the difficulties normally encountered in family research. It will rely on a common sense approach to research problems, tossing out some homespun hints and suggestions here and there where appropriate. Each and every twist and turn in family research cannot, of course, be foreseen, so the reader is advised to keep his ear to the ground and his weather eye open!

Questions Often Asked

In practice our visitors' efforts at tracing their ancestors are marked by a hesitancy which stems from a lack of guidance. 'Should we go first to the parish or should we begin our search in the city?' 'Will we be able to find Ballybeg?' Does the church still exist?' 'Where are the records kept?' 'Are there road signs?' Are there any interesting places we should see while in the country?' 'Who should we talk to locally?' 'What about guide books and maps?'

Getting Started

'Where should we start?' is a question frequently asked by overseas visitors to Ireland intent on learning something about their Irish forebears. The answer to this question is simple. If you happen to be in the city, the place to start is the city. If you happen to be in the country, in or near the supposed place of origin of your ancestors, then the place to start is the country. However, depending on where a start is made to a search care must be taken to use the appropriate search technique.

Dublin

Let's say, for example sake, you commence your search in Dublin, home of the country's biggest libraries and record offices. These literary storehouses contain the raw materials from which you may hope to forge your family tree. The records were, of course, made at a particular point in time in the past, usually for a specific purpose and hopefully, from your point of view, enough of them still survive to enable you to learn something about your particular family.

Birthdates

Usually some elementary and commonsense mathematics will be called for. Thus a birthdate may have to be fixed by reference to age at death. The probable date of a marriage may have to be calculated from the birthdates of the children. The exact date of emigration of an ancestor will have to be established, and so on. Precise dating is always a key element in the documentary approach to tracing ancestors. When using this technique the standard method of proceeding is to start with the informant and work backwards to the preceding generation and then back to the more remote generations.

Local Tradition

The exact opposite approach must be adopted when tapping local tradition for information about bygone generations. The oral tradition technique is normally employed on the occasion of a visit to the locality of one's ancestors. A local narrator of family lore will usually take as his starting point the founding ancestor of the family inquired about many generations back. As a general rule the founding ancestor will have been born sometime between 1780 and 1830, depending on the age of the narrator and the generational depth of the tradition he carries.

First the names of the children of the founding ancestor will be recited. Then one of those children will be chosen and his children named and so on down the generations until the present day descendants are reached.

Traditional Recitation of Genealogies

The listener to a traditional recitation of genealogies is frequently perplexed by the apparent failure on the part of the narrator to give dates of christenings and weddings of the old people, i.e. ancestors. True, the precise 'day and month' dating system which is such a standard feature of the documentary approach is alien to the oral tradition technique of tracing ancestors. Nevertheless the generations are clearly marked by reference to events which may be of national, local or climatic significance. Thus, for example, 1832 will be spoken of in terms of 'the year of the Terrible Fever'; 1839 was 'the year of the Big Wind'; 1847 'the year of the Famine'; 1848 'the year of Smith-O'Brien' (of Young Ireland Rebellion fame); 1857 'the year of the Big Frost'; 1867 'the year of the Fenians' and so on.

Devotion to detail will be evident from the manner in which the narrator carefully localises each homestead — at the crossroads, near the railway line, above the chapel, or at the bottom of the hill. A change in the ownership of a farm whether through purchase or inheritance is clearly enunciated, as well as the succession of owners should a particular property happen to have changed hands.

The O's and the Mac's

Overseas visitors researching their family origins occasionally have difficulty in coming to terms with Irish surname prefixes — what local people call the 'O's' and the 'Mac's'. If we glance at the 1981 Irish Telephone Directory, Part 2, under the letter 'O' covering the Republic but excluding Dublin City and its environs, we observe column after column of entries relating to well-known Irish names such as O'Brien, O'Connor, O'Byrne, O'Callaghan, O'Carroll, O'Doherty, and so on down the alphabet to O'Toole.

Further interspersed between these blocks of names we also observe some entries for names like Oakes, Odlum, Olden, Ormond, Osbourne and Owens. It is evident that the initial 'O' of these latter names — all of English origin — is an integral element of the name whereas the 'O' of O'Brien, O'Connor, O'Dempsey, etc. stands apart as a distinct word in its own right.

Meaning of O-

The Irish surname prefix 'O' is simply the standard English form of the Gaelic word *Ua* — roughly pronounced 'Awe' — meaning 'descendant'. Thus the O'Sullivans represent a surname group whose members would claim descent from a remote ancestor, i.e. *Suildubháin,* believed to have flourished in the 9th century. That descent, in the case of an individual member of the group, might be in the male or female line, or through marriage or simply because he happened to be born in the territory of the O'Sullivans. The Irish word 'clan' and the English word 'sept' are often used to describe a large surname group like the O'Sullivans.

Dropping of O-

Over the past two centuries there has been a progressive tendency to drop the prefix 'O' from Irish surnames. Confirmation of this trend can readily be found in the edition of the Irish Telephone Directory cited above. To take a couple of significant examples: there are only some 100 entries under O'Kelly as opposed to over 2,000 under Kelly; O'Ryan is limited to a mere five entries while, by contrast, Ryan has approximately 3,000. On the other hand Connell, Donovan and Sullivan are, in terms of usage, minority forms of these names, since the great majority of members of these families continue to style themselves O'Connell, O'Donovan and O'Sullivan.

Meaning of Mac & Mc

The other well-known Irish surname prefix — also used by the Scots — is, of course, Mac, frequently shortened to Mc, meaning 'son'. The Irish Telephone Directory (Part Two) devotes about 65 pages to 'Mac' surnames. 'O' and 'Mac', it should be noted, are part and parcel of a long standing surname system which is invariably used in official records, church registers and gravestone inscriptions. Because of the tendency to drop and assume these prefixes care should be taken when 'looking up' indexes to surnames to check under both the basic and prefixed versions of the surname, e.g. Sweeney/McSweeney, Rourke/O'Rourke.

Surnames — New & Old

What the Telephone Directory shows is that there is a hard core of ancient names that persist in Ireland; that many of these are 'high frequency' names and that some tend to be associated with certain parts of the country. Additionally, there are a great many scattered 'low frequency' names mainly of English and Scottish origin arising out of the plantation settlements of the 17th century.

Christian Name Pattern in the Generations

We now come to take a look at the system widely used by Irish parents in the 19th century of choosing Christian names for their children. The tradition strictly adhered to in many parts of Ireland was that the father named the first-born after his father or mother and the mother the second-born after her father or mother. They then alternated until both sets of parental names were used up. Then they used the names of their brothers and sisters — *always alternating*.

System of Naming the Generations

Under the system a child's Christian name linked him with his grandparental generation and the names used were usually drawn from the pool of names in use in that generation. The eldest children in particular were firmly linked to their grandparents' generation and thus an *alternating generation* cycle of Christian names was established. So, if the names of the children of the emigrant ancestor in the order in which they were born are known it should be possible to reconstruct the names of the parental generation of that ancestor. This kind of projection can give purpose and direction to a search, particularly where birth and baptismal records are concerned.

Example	Likely names of the parents of John Kelly:	William Kelly & Kathleen —
	Emigrant Ancestor:	John Kelly, emigrated to New York circa 1849.
	Children of Emigrant Ancestor:	William, Thomas, Kathleen, James, Mary

Assuming that John Kelly was approximately 20 years of age when he emigrated, a thorough search of church registers for his baptismal entry should span the period 1829 $\pm$ 5 years, i.e. 1824-1834.

The Naming of the Land

The Irish people have been inclined to lavish names on their land. There is scarcely a rock or clump of trees or path that goes unnamed. Each of the fields comprising a farm has its own name, e.g. the river field, the chapel field, the road field, the coursing field, the bush field, the nine acres and so on. Ten or fifteen contiguous farms go to make a townland — the smallest administrative unit of land in Ireland.

Townland

The geographic term 'townland' arose from an unfortunate official translation of the Gaelic *baile fearainn* meaning 'homestead land'. There is here no question of a township or urban centre of any kind. The confusion probably arose because of a later and secondary meaning ascribed to the word *baile* — usually rendered 'Bally' in the English language — equating it with 'village', 'town' and 'city'. The place-name prefix 'Bally--' occurs in about 6,500 townlands or one in every ten townlands in Ireland. Other high frequency townland prefixes include *Cill* — Kill, meaning a church; *Cnoc* — Knock, a hill; *Lios* — Lis(s), a rath or fort and *Doire* — Derry, an oak wood.

Townland Names: Local Versions

A word of caution here. There was a tendency on the part of local people to disregard common townland prefixes in everyday speech. This practice occasionally gave rise to a popular and an official version of the same townland name. Thus, for example, a particular townland may be known in local circles as 'Lough' whereas the same townland would be listed as Ballylough in Government registers and other official records.

Townland Names: Official Versions

Our townlands bespeak the names of local families, man-made structures such as churches and fortifications, features of the landscape like woods, streams, hills etc., historical events and mythical allusions. In size they vary greatly, a goodly number falling in the range of 50 to 500 acres. Twenty or thirty adjacent townlands grouped round an abbey or church (nowadays often in ruins) go to make a parish.

Parish

From the time of the Reformation in the 16th century down to the present day the Irish Church has been organised on the basis of two separate parochial structures, one Catholic, the other Protestant. Since Protestantism was the official religion of the State, the Protestant parish, in addition to this obvious function as a unit of ecclesiastical administration, was also employed as a unit of civil administration for the purposes of census taking and tithe composition. Catholic parishes, on the other hand, were used solely for ecclesiastical purposes and generally were larger than their Protestant counterparts. Each denomination maintained its own registers of baptisms and marriages; the surviving original volumes are held in presbyteries and churches throughout the country.

Barony

In addition to the townland and parish there is a further entity or should we say administrative oddity that must be reckoned with particularly by those looking to the records to throw some light on past generations. That entity is known as the barony. Unlike the townland and parish which continue to function as organic units, the barony, as a unit of administration has been obsolete for almost a century. Nevertheless between 1600 and 1900 the barony was used extensively by the English administration in Ireland as a convenient unit in the making of land surveys and population counts.

Barony Names

Although the barony is a Norman term, nevertheless the names of many of the baronies eloquently bespeak the territorial holdings of the great old Irish families, for example, Clanmaurice, Oneillands, Tirkennedy, Clankelly and Iraghticonnor.

Towns & Villages as Points of Local Reference

As you drive through the countryside directional signposts at each crossroads beckon you to the next town or village: Castlecomer or Castleconnell or Castleisland is but a mere 5 miles or 8 kilometres distant. It is important to remember that our towns and villages are natural points of reference as far as local people are concerned: the location of a townland, for example, will often be given by reference to the nearest town or village.

The Ordnance Survey, Phoenix Park, Dublin has published a set of five sectional maps of the entire country: the names and locations of most Irish towns and villages are clearly marked on these maps.

To the Country in Search of Ancestors

In the countryside when endeavouring to trace a grandparent or great grandparent what you need most of all is a sense of purpose and direction. You should be prepared to make a clear and simple statement of the known facts in your own particular case whenever the occasion demands. Avoid, as far as possible, the use of words like 'ancestor' and 'ancestry': to the ears of many country people such terms smack of remote generations beyond recall. Instead it is preferable to use the more meaningful phrase. . . my people came from. . . Likewise the clumsy and abstract term 'genealogy' should be discarded in favour of the practical and colloquial 'tracing relationships'. It is essential to have in one's possession a clear map, preferably one showing townlands, of the area to be visited as well as, of course, a notebook and pen. Nearly always there is one individual in a locality who is recognised to be an authority on the history of local families. In the course of conversation with locals you should always be on the alert for the identity of the 'local historian'.

Local Visit

It will be appreciated that Saturdays and Sundays are not the most appropriate days to select for a visit to a local parish church because of the heavier pastoral commitments of clergy on weekends. Whichever day you choose to visit the locale of your ancestors you should signify your intentions well in advance by writing to the local clergyman, clearly stating your requirements in so far as they relate to his registers. The names, addresses and telephone numbers of the clergy will be found listed in current Church directories. You should address your letter to The Rev. Parish Priest (R. Catholic), The Rev. Rector (Church of Ireland) or the Rev. Minister,

(Presbyterian) as appropriate, followed by the full address as given in the directories. (See Useful books, page 32).

Local Institutions

In Ireland as elsewhere no doubt life in country districts revolves round a number of well defined local institutions. As focal points of communication, the church, school, post office, public house, parish magazine and local newspaper all have some potential to shed light on bygone generations. The question is this — how can a visitor to Ireland best utilise these institutions in order to learn more about the particular family in which he or she has a personal interest?

Local Library

The local branch library is one of the best points of departure for hitting the ancestor trail in the country. Usually there is one reasonably close at hand. What they do not have they can borrow for you to consult through the inter-library loan arrangement. Moreover, they are more likely, than say the larger libraries, to retain copies of parish bulletins, newsletters and magazines. A local historian will nearly always deposit a copy of his research in the local branch library. A list of the branch libraries in the various counties is given on page 28.

Post Office

As the post office is, of course, the mailing centre for a locality the postmaster or postmistress is bound to be a knowledgeable person on matters like the names and addresses of people living in the countryside roundabout. A simple inquiry at the post office counter as to the cost of sending a card home to Tulsa, Toronto or Tasmania provides a ready made opportunity to strike up a conversation with these knowledgeable local officials.

It is well to remember, too, that on Fridays senior citizens in the locality make their way to the post office to collect the old age pension and one or two of these hardy seventy and eighty year olds are certain to possess long memories.

The names of all post offices in Ireland are contained in an official post office guide available from The Government Publications Sales Office, G.P.O. Arcade, Dublin 1.

Baptismal Records

Each new-born arrival in a parish — often sponsored by old survivors — is introduced initially into the community at baptism: *Ego te baptizo in nomine*

A Companion Guide

Patris et Filii et Spiritus Sancti. A record of the ceremony is then made in the parish register:

1839 die 6 Jan. Ego Rev. J. O'Brien baptizavi Patricium filium legitimum Joannis McCarthy et Mariae Walsh de Karrigeen. Sponsores Daniel et Brigida Murphy.

The register is usually kept at the home of the clergyman or in a small room off the Church known as the Vestry or Sacristy.

Content of Parish Registers

When reading a parish register a person should constantly bear in mind that he or she is thumbing and leafing a unique manuscript — a local Book of Kells, you might say. The reader will find that older parish registers tend to be written in the Latin language, with records of baptisms and marriages entered in the same volume. From the 1840's onward separate registers were kept for baptisms and for marriages. Since clergymen, like other mortals come and go, parish registers were (and still are, of course) compiled by several hands, some in the finest copperplate, others difficult enough to read. Occasionally a new priest or incumbent may alter the layout of entries but this need not unduly slow the progress of the careful reader of parish registers.

Age of Parish Registers

Now for a question that must agitate the minds of people at home and abroad contemplating an odyssey into their families' past — how far back do Irish parish registers go? The answer to this question may be summarised as follows:—

Parishes	Registers begin
Cities and larger towns	1750 (approx.)
Market towns and areas with a literary tradition	1775 (approx.)
Country areas	1800-1825 (approx.)

For a printed source giving earliest starting dates of Irish parish registers — Roman Catholic, Church of Ireland (Protestant) and Presbyterian (Protestant) the reader should turn to Useful Books, page 32.

Checking Parish Registers

On arrival you should endeavour to make the acquaintance of the parish clerk whose responsibilities include the care and maintenance of the local

Ireland

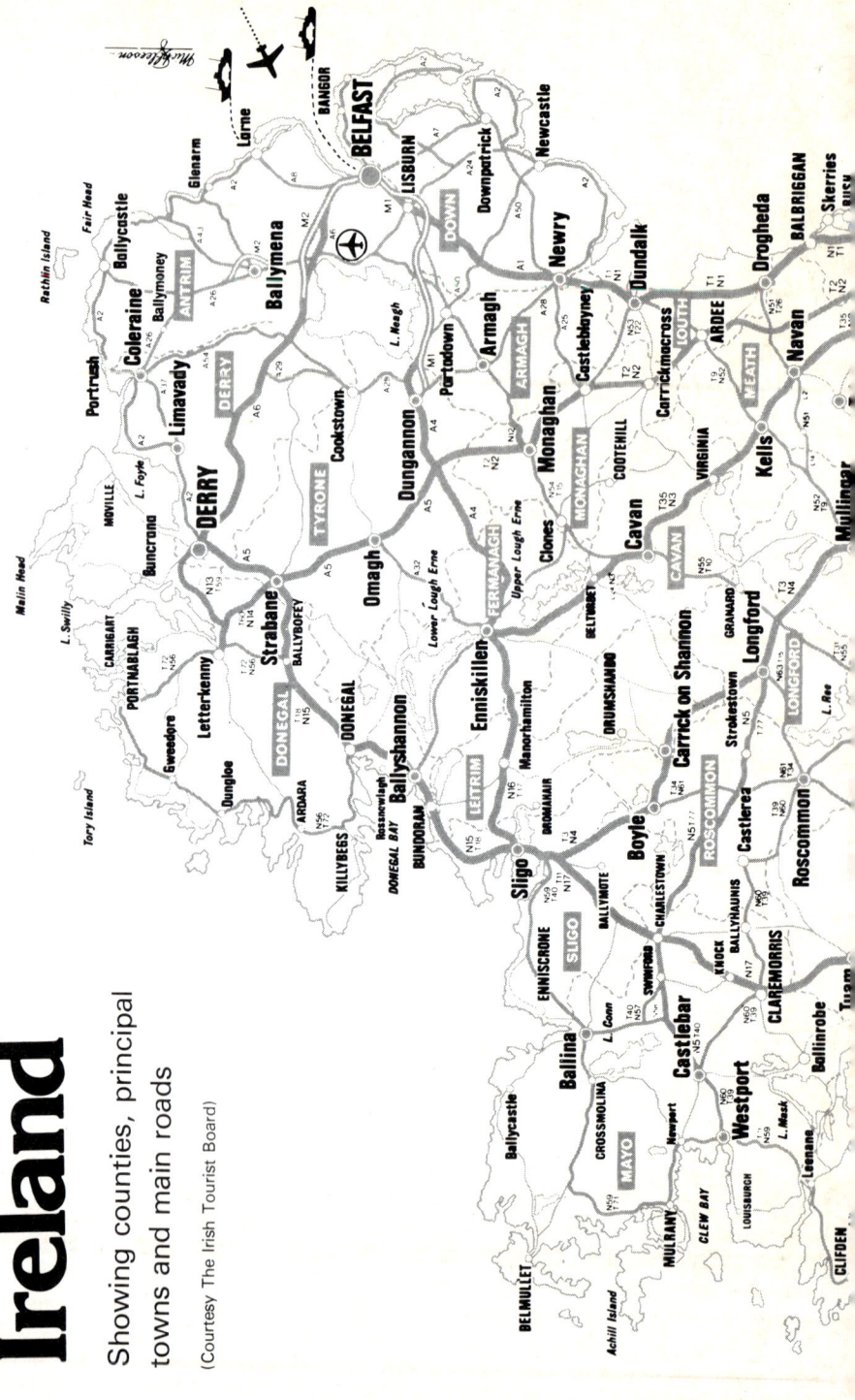

Showing counties, principal towns and main roads

(Courtesy The Irish Tourist Board)

17

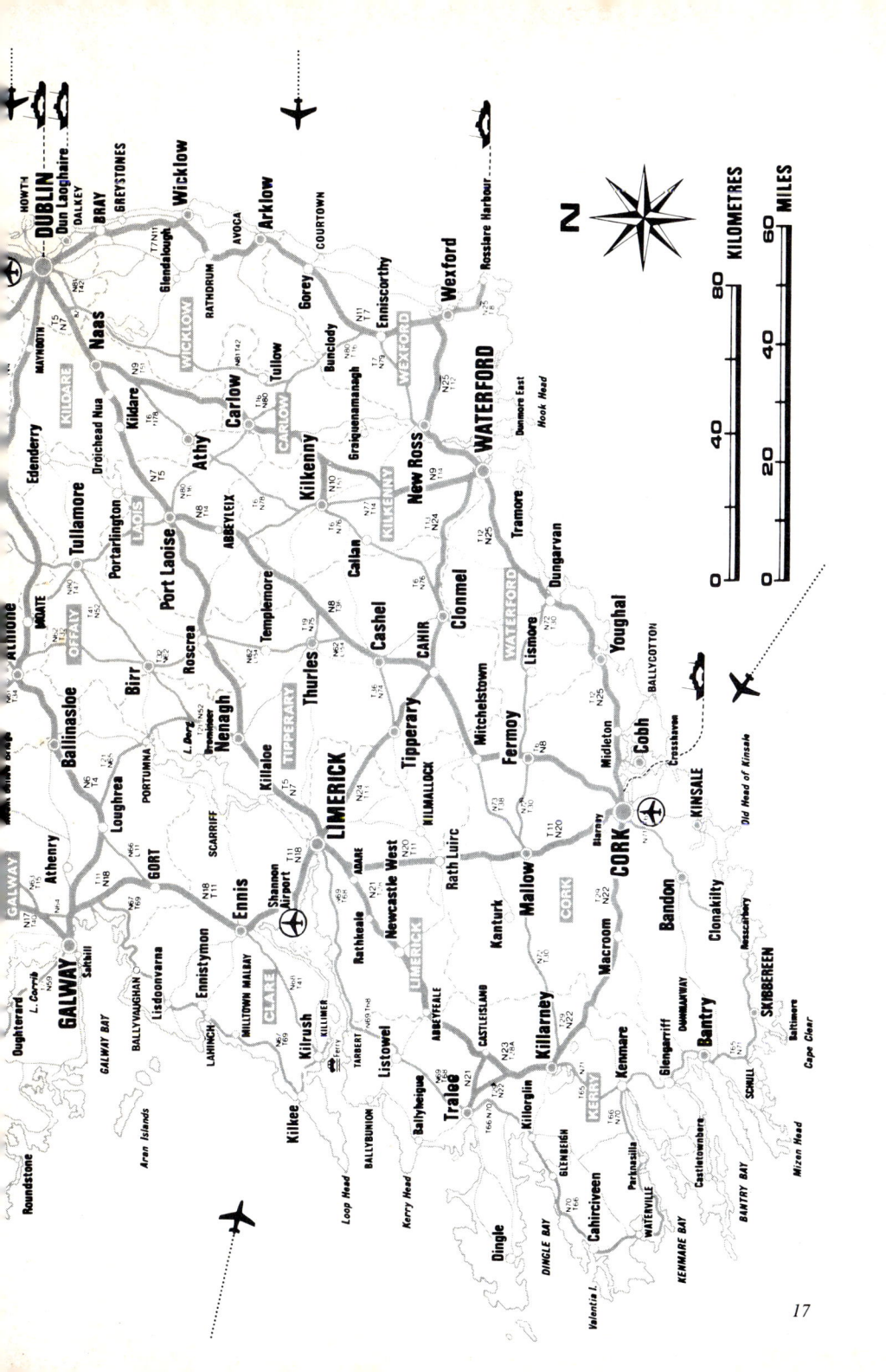

church. Of course, any child in the locality will be able to point unerringly to the site of the church and the presbytery. It is a good idea to pin on the notice board in the church a short query, preferably preprepared and typed, seeking information about your ancestor, not forgetting to add your name and home address. If for one reason or another the parish priest is not at home, you should, in that event, make an arrangement with the parish clerk to procure on your behalf, from the parish priest, a letter authorising you to consult the copies of his registers held in central archives in Dublin and Belfast. This requirement, it should be noted, is now no longer necessary in the case of registers of parishes in the following dioceses:

> Achonry, Armagh, Clogher, Clonfert, Cork & Ross, Derry, Dromore, Dublin, Elphin, Ferns, Killala, Killaloe, Kilmore, Meath, Ossory, Raphoe, Tuam, Waterford & Lismore.

Living Relatives

Linked to their efforts to ascertain the facts about past generations is the natural and understandable desire on the part of many of our visitors to discover the whereabouts of any living relatives they may still have in Ireland. A search for present-day descendants of say a brother or sister of an 19th century emigrant can be conducted only at local level and one of the best aids in that task is the current register of electors.

Register of Electors

This register of electors is compiled on a county basis and is revised annually. The register purports to list all those who are entitled to vote in Irish elections, that is to say, persons over eighteen years of age. The names of those entitled to vote are set out in ABC order under the townlands where they reside. Persons in the same household are listed consecutively — so it is possible to tell at a glance the set of christian names in everyday use by a particular family. The *district* electoral section of the register may be read at the local branch library, the Garda (Police) Station and the post office.

County and Local Newspapers

Despite their best efforts in their home countries it often happens that overseas visitors to Ireland are unable to uncover any information beyond the fact that their ancestor was born in a particular Irish county. Rather than face the doubtful prospect of a long search through all parishes in the county in question it might be preferable, for a start, to write to the Editor of the local or county newspaper. You should, of course, use your home address when writing to the Editor who no doubt would be anxious to prove to his readers how widespread the circulation of his paper is. Letters should be short, clearly giving what information is known about an ancestor and requesting from readers any information they may have to offer. A list of county and local newspapers is printed on page 30 of this publication.

Local Publications

In recent years local history, in which genealogy and family lore play a vital part, has been gaining in popular appeal in the countryside. More and more parish histories issue from the press each year while the parish magazine is now a welcome feature in a growing number of parishes around the country. The editor of a parish magazine is certain to relish a human story that links the little village with the world beyond the seas. When going to see the editor it is an advantage to have on one's person one or two old photographs of the emigrant ancestor and his family in their adopted country. Often the editor of the parish magazine is a local teacher which, incidentally, suggests yet a further line of inquiry at local, namely school records.

School Records

In 1831 the English administration in Ireland established a state system of elementary education for the entire country. The administration and implementation of the National Schools in Ireland generated a large volume of records including, naturally enough, school registers and roll books.

School registers normally contain the following particulars: name, age and date of entry into the school of the pupil, parents' names, their address and occupation.

The large dreary folios full of dots and dashes that comprise the school rolls are not so informative although they do list the register number of the pupil, his name and record of attendance.

Occasionally the age of a scholar will be neatly inserted after his name on the school roll: thus we find that Lawrence McManus and William Reilly were both aged 17 years and in fourth class in Trim (Co. Meath) National School in 1855.

The main problem relating to the use of school records for family research is to establish whether the registers of a particular school still exist, and if so where such registers can be consulted. Unfortunately, as far as can be ascertained, surviving school records are rather scattered. It is known that some are held in the Department of Education and some in the Public Record Office, Dublin. Many more are in local custody either retained in the schools themselves or deposited along with parish registers in the churches.

Headstones

(Headstone illustration: "TILL THE DAY BREAK AND THE SHADOWS FLEET AWAY")

The practice in Ireland of erecting headstones in the open to mark the exact position of burials is not much older than 1725. The type of stone used for marking the place of burial was of the variety plentiful in the locality, generally limestone, each slab being positioned at the head of the grave, facing eastward. Because of their orientation, inscriptions on headstones have escaped the worst effects of weathering caused by our prevalent south-westerlies. Since many of these inscriptions provide data, not elsewhere available, on the older generations of families, they ought not, for that reason, be overlooked on the occasion of a local visit.

Local Assistance

The average country churchyard will have between 150 and 300 upright stones. So, it is not advisable for a stranger to attempt to isolate the family headstone sought because this task unaided can only be accomplished through a process of elimination. Better by far to enlist the assistance of a sympathetic local soul, preferably an older person, who after directing you to the site of the cemetery, will often be able to point to the exact plots of individual families.

The ground around the medieval parish church in many instances is still in use to this day as the parish burial-place. The oldest headstones will be found to be located south of the now ruined church as people had an aversion to being buried in the part of the cemetery facing the north. Dare we say that even in consecrated christian ground the Celtic prejudices of the pagani or countrymen never died!

Reading Headstone Inscriptions

Reading an inscription on a headstone will occasionally prove difficult which is not surprising in view of the age of some of the stones. If the stone is clear of ivy and lichen a handful of young green grass rubbed vigorously along the line of the inscription will draw out the incised lettering. Another reading technique employed is to chalk the area of the inscription using the elongated flat surface of a piece of white chalk. The stone is then fanned say with a newspaper in order to remove surplus chalk powder. The incised portions of the stone will receive less chalk with the result that the somewhat darker inscription should contrast with the immediate whiter area of the headstone. The chalk will quickly disappear after rain and no damage will come to the stone.

If the stone is ivy-clad the ivy may be removed by hand strand by strand using a minimum of force, thereby enabling an interested party to read any inscription such a stone may carry. Stones affected by lichen growth generally present a distinctive grey appearance: stones so affected require special treatment before a reading can be attempted. Instructions in regard to the treatment of lichen on headstones are given below.

One parting word! Although a family may have resided in a particular parish over a number of generations they may not in fact be buried in the parish cemetery at all. Instead members of the family elect to be buried in a neighbouring parish cemetery, a sure pointer to the remoter origins of such a family.

Treatment of Lichen on Headstones

1. Mix one part of commercial formaldehyde with five parts of clean water and spray the surface of the stone sufficiently only to wet it.

2. The surface must not be scrubbed or brushed in any way.

3. Rain following within half an hour of spraying may reduce the effectiveness of the treatment.

4. The effect of this treatment takes about six months to become apparent and the stone will usually become perfectly clean in twelve to eighteen months.

5. The treatment is more effective on stonework exposed to sunlight than on stonework in a poor light.

6. The initial treatment may be repeated after one to six months, if the discolouration of the stone is very bad.

7. The spray is non-poisonous to animals or people, but it is irritating to the eyes and to some extent to the skin, so that protective clothing should be worn by the operator.

Searching the Records: A Checklist

☐ **Records of Births, Marriages and Deaths**

Records of births, marriages and deaths are a key source for information on past generations. The civil registration of vital statistics did not become the general practice in Ireland until 1864. Before that date the only source for such information is church records — with one exception. That exception is Church of Ireland (Protestant) marriages which were subject to civil registration from April, 1845.

Under the registration acts of 1863 to 1972 the Registrar-General issues certificates of births, marriages and deaths based on the registers held at his office.

A birth certificate will state the date and exact place of birth, the name given to the child, also the name, surname and place of dwelling of the father as well as the maiden name of the mother.

A marriage certificate will state the names of the parties, date and place of marriage, the residence of each at the time of the marriage, and interestingly, the names of the fathers of both parties to the marriage.

A death certificate is the least informative of these documents, merely stating the name, age and place of death of the deceased.

The General Registrar's Office is located at 8-11 Lombard Street East, Dublin and is open to the public.

☐ **Parish Registers**

Parish registers are among the most useful documentary sources a family researcher can use but in order to be effective the religious denomination and parish of the ancestor sought must be known. In Ireland two separate and ongoing sets of registers, one Catholic, the other Protestant, will be found to exist side by side for most parishes as a consequence of the parallel parochial structure of the Irish Church from the Reformation onwards. A catalogue, arranged by county, of most of the surviving registers of the three main Christian denominations in Ireland — Roman Catholic, Church of Ireland and Presbyterian — and specifying the year of the commencement of each register, is printed in *Handbook on Irish Genealogy,* 6th ed., 1984, pages 75-89 (see Useful Books page 32).

☐ Voters Lists

In Ireland the register of electors is compiled on a county basis. For electoral purposes each county is divided into a number of large units known as County Electoral Areas. Each of these in turn is subdivided into smaller areas known as District Electoral Divisions.

The register of electors is constantly reviewed since only those whose names appear on the register are entitled to vote. The register which is a useful proof that a person was alive and resident in a certain place at the time in question can be inspected in county and local branch libraries.

☐ Wills

Wills are obviously of great interest to those employing the documentary approach to tracing their Irish ancestors. While the odd notoriously bogus will comes to light from time to time the vast majority of wills may be regarded as genuine documents full of reliable and useful genealogical information. In addition to the names of the testators, witnesses and executors, wills normally give the names of spouse and children and any other parties standing to benefit from the provisions of a will.

For those hoping to trace the existence of any wills made by their ancestors the appropriate office is the Public Record Office, Dublin. The Card Index in the Search Room there is reckoned to list about 20,000 or so wills and other testamentary items up to the year 1857. From 1858 onwards there is a printed alphabetically arranged yearly calendar to wills and administrations. The Calendar entries give the name, address and occupation of the deceased as well as the place and exact date of death. These Calendars are kept in the Search Room.

For a comprehensive account of Irish Wills and Administrations from a genealogical point of view the reader is referred to *Irish Genealogy: A Record Finder,* Chapter 6. (see Useful Books).

☐ Tithe Listings

In 1823 an act passed in the English Parliament decreed that tithes due to the Established Church in Ireland be paid in money rather than in kind as had been the case previous to that date. The new method of tithe payment called for an assessment of the entire country, parish by parish. In the course of that assessment the pecuniary amount of tithe payable by each individual holder of land was fixed based on the average price received for grain in each parish over the seven years preceding 1828. The returns of this assessment form what are popularly known as the Tithe Books.

The Tithe Books, numbering in all about 2,000 hand-written volumes, range in date from 1823 to 1837. Each parish tithe book is set down in tabular form under the following principal headings: townland, names of occupiers of that townland, acreage held, quality of the land and rent paid. The tithe lists form the first comprehensive register of people in relation to the tenancy of the land of Ireland. They are all the more important from a genealogical point of view because of the destruction of the 1821 census.

The tithe returns for the Republic are in the keeping of the Public Record Office, Dublin. The books for the six counties of Northern Ireland are kept in the Public Record Office of Northern Ireland, Belfast. It should be noted, however, that microform copies of the northern books are available at the National Library of Ireland, Kildare St., Dublin.

☐ Rateable Valuation Returns

The Tenement Act of 1852 provided for one uniform valuation of all property in Ireland based on the productive capacity of the land and the economic rent of buildings. The purpose of the valuation was to establish a fair and equitable basis upon which to levy local taxation. It was at this period our forefathers first 'paid the rates'. The valuation was conducted by the prominent Dublin geologist Richard Griffith and so is often referred to as Griffith's Valuation. The work of valuation was begun in 1848 and completed for the entire country in 1864. The returns ran to over 200 printed books, one for each barony. The particulars given include the name of the individual property holder, his town land or street address, the name of his immediate landlord, a description of his holding, as well as, of course, details of the Valuation Official's findings. Only the major Irish libraries and record offices would have a complete printed set of the printed valuation returns although each county library should have the returns covering its own county.

☐ Incumbered Estates Records

In the immediate aftermath of the Famine an estimated two million persons were in receipt of poor-law relief; local taxation levies equalled about half the received rental of the country and the population was decreasing at the rate of half a million a year. Small wonder that the estates of the landed class, deprived of their rent revenues, began to sink beyond redemption in incumbrances of every kind. An avalanche of petitions from mortgagees and receivers seeking foreclosure orders on estates proved too much for the ordinary courts to handle. Accordingly in 1850 the Government was forced to establish a special court known as the Incumbered Estates Court to deal with bankrupt estates.

The petitioner's case for 'an order of sale' to the Incumbered Estates Court involved the preparation, in the words of a contemporary source, 'of a

A Companion Guide

handsome folio volume, elegantly printed, and copiously illustrated with lithographic plans, vividly-coloured drawings, sections, and elevations, together with tabulated columns, showing the tenancies, rents, and acreage — in short, such a complete topographical picture in one volume — of his estate as must have astonished the Incumbered Nobleman himself.'

In the lifespan of the Court (1850-1858) some 8,000 estates were sold, an illustrated topographical memoir of each such estate having been presented to the Court for its information.

In 1858 a new court under the title of the Landed Estates Court was established to deal with unincumbered as well as incumbered estates.

The detailed particulars in the printed folios presented to both these courts are of considerable value in 19th century family research in view of the large numbers of ordinary people who were tenants on the affected estates.

It is doubtful if there is a complete set of these folios now in existence; the National Library of Ireland has probably the most complete run 1837-1896. They also have an index covering the years 1850-1864.

☐ **Owners of Land**

In 1873 following an order in the English Parliament a survey of land owners was undertaken in Ireland. The findings of that survey entitled *Returns of the Owners of Land* was published in Dublin in 1876. Only those who owned one acre and upwards were taken into account in the survey. The returns show the names of such owners arranged in ABC order for each county. Additionally the address of the owner, the extent of his holding and the amount of valuation were tabulated in each case.

Appended to the returns is a further list of the names of proprietors in the several counties of Ireland holding areas of land ranging in size from 20,000 acres downwards to 25 acres.

The *Returns of Owners of Land* affords the reader an interesting summary of the position in the country relating to the ownership of land following the crash of the great estates in the post-famine years.

☐ **Registration of Land**

Many transactions involving the sale, lease and mortgage of land have been formally recorded at the Registry of Deeds, Henrietta St., Dublin from 1708 onwards. The records of the Registry clearly mirror the situation in relation to the ownership of land in Ireland in the 18th and 19th centures. The majority of registered transactions relate to the landed gentry and substantial farmer classes; small farmers and tenants rarely figure in the records of the Registry. The records of the Registry of Deeds and how best to use those records are discussed in *Irish Genealogy: A Record Finder,* Chapter 7. (See Useful Books, page 32).

Seven Wonders of Ireland

New Grange
Over 5,000 years ago our remote ancestors constructed a number of megalithic monuments in the Boyne Valley which to this day continue to baffle antiquarians, archaeologists and ordinary people alike. What, for instance, was the original purpose of the mounds at New Grange, Knowth and Dowth and how are we to interpret the rock carvings that characterize these mounds? Are these patently geometrical forms merely decorative, or are they symbolic, or do they constitute an organised and meaningful system of communication? These questions are the subject of ongoing excavation and research which have generated a considerable volume of literature. New Grange and the other ancient structures lie close to the village of Slane, Co. Meath and regular tours are conducted on the site.

Great Skellig
Like some imposing cathedral the *Great Skellig* rises from the sea eight miles out from Bolus Head in the Iveragh peninsula in south-west Co. Kerry. So perfectly preserved is the entire original foundation that one can almost sense here the beginnings of the Christian experience in Ireland. In this remarkable place little more than a hundred years after the death of St. Patrick, a lesser known saint, Fionan by name, founded a monastic settlement. There is a long tradition of pilgrimage associated with this settlement and it is perhaps in that spirit a visit to the island is best undertaken. The journey to the *Greak Skellig* (on a fine day only) takes about forty minutes from Portmagee or Cahirciveen, Co. Kerry.

Clonmacnois
Clonmacnois, that great centre of learning founded by St. Kieran in 547 lies beside the River Shannon nine miles downstream from Athlone. Whether one approaches this tranquil place by road or river Clonmacnois looks impressive by reason of the fact that it retains many tangible remains of its former greatness. In addition to its two well preserved round towers, there are two finely carved stone crosses, eight churches, two holy wells and more than 200 burial flagstones inscribed with old Gaelic names. In order to profit fully from a visit to Clonmacnois it is advisable to join one of the guided tours provided during the holiday season.

Bunratty Castle and Folk Park
Whether your people in the past were kings or simply king's men, estate owners or impoverished tenants, townspeople or country folk, farmers or fishermen, Bunratty Castle and Folk Museum affords a unique insight into the lifestyle of your Irish forebears particularly in the 19th century. The castle itself, originally the home of the McNamaras and later one of the principal strongholds of the O'Briens, has been arranged as the chief seat of a great Irish family would have been five hundred years ago. Visitors to the Folk Park step straight into the living past. All around them the domestic and village life of bygone generations is lived to the full. The traditional crafts and trades of nineteenth century Ireland such as those of the blacksmith, the basketmaker, the thatcher and the thresher are plainly practised for all to see. Truly it can be said that the Folk Park is a window on the past. Bunratty Castle and Folk Park is situated about six miles from Shannon International Airport on the main Limerick to Ennis road. It is open to visitors all the year round and guidebooks can be purchased on location for a nominal sum.

Kilkenny City

People who desire to sample the atmosphere of ancient, medieval and modern Ireland in a *single* location will find that Kilkenny City provides them with an opportunity to do just that.

This ancient city, situated on the banks of the River Nore, with its civil and ecclesiastical roots deep in the past, combines an air of old-world charm with the progressiveness of today.

Saint Canice, after whom the city is named, built a 6th century church on the site now occupied by St. Canice's Cathedral. After the Anglo-Norman invasion in 1170 the town was granted to Strongbow, Earl of Pembroke. From 1203 to 1408 the city was the venue of many parliaments and in 1642 it became the seat of the Confederate Parliament, representing the Irish and Anglo-Norman Catholics, which functioned for six years.

Kilkenny city is currently the focal point of a growing craft and design movement. There are 35 small craft industries based in the area.

What To See in Kilkenny is the subject of a number of brochures produced by the local tourist office located at Shee Alms House, Rose Inn Street.

Trinity College, Dublin

The atmosphere of the College, founded by Elizabeth I in 1592, is probably best appreciated when the university is in session. Here is an oasis of scholarship and learning located at the centre of the business orientated metropolis.

The Long Room is one of the oldest surviving buildings in the College and houses the Books of Kells and the 'Brian Boru' harp as well as a host of other reminders of Ireland's cultural past.

Information leaflets in English, French and German are available at the College and are of considerable assistance in finding one's way around the campus.

Cultra

The function of the Ulster folk museum at Cultra is to present a view of the traditional way of life of people resident in the northern part of Ireland over the past couple of centuries. In Cultra Manor, the focus of an old landed estate, the galleries exhibit a large range of objects associated with the traditional life-style of the northern province. In the open air folk park there is a selection of buildings removed from all parts of Ulster and re-erected at Cultra in settings as close as possible to the originals. There is also a transport museum with interesting exhibits illustrating the development of means of transport in Ireland.

The Ulster Folk and Transport Museum is sited at Cultra, Holywood, Co. Down and illustrated information packs are available at the centre.

Seeing the Wonders of Ireland

Ireland is an uncomplicated country to visit. It is easily accessible by direct air services and it offers all the facilities visitors require. Further information on visiting Ireland is available from the Irish Tourist Board or Aer Lingus, the Irish Airline, who maintain offices in most of the major cities of the world. Postal enquiries should be sent to the Irish Tourist Board, P.O. Box 273, Dublin 8.

County and Branch Libraries

The address of the principal library in each county is followed by the locations of the branch libraries in that county.

Antrim: Demesne Avenue, Ballymena, BT43 7BG.
   Ahoghill, Antrim, Ballee, Ballycastle, Ballymena, Ballymoney, Broughshane, Bushmills, Carrickfergus, Castlerock, Cloghmills, Crumlin, Dunmurry, Fernagh, Glengormley, Greenisland, Greystone, Larne, Lisburn, Monkstown, Portrush, Randalstown, Rathcoole, Templepatrick, Twinbrook, Whitehead.

Armagh: Brownlow Row, Legahory, Craigavon, BT65 8DP.
   Armagh, Bessbrook, Craigavon, Keady, Lurgan, Portadown, Tandragee.

Carlow: Dublin Street, Carlow.
   Carlow, Muinebheag, Tullow.

Cavan: Casement Street, Cavan.
   Arva, Bailieboro, Ballinagh, Ballyconnell, Ballyjamesduff, Belturbet, Cootehill, Kileshandra, Kingscourt, Kilnaleck, Virginia.

Clare: Mill Road, Ennis.
   Corofin, Ennis, Ennistymon, Kildysart, Killaloe, Kilrush, Lisdoonvarna, Miltown Malbay, Newmarket-on-Fergus, Scariff, Shannon, Sixmilebridge, Tulla.

Cork: The Courthouse, Washington Street, Cork.
   Ballincollig, Ballydehob, Bandon, Bantry, Buttevant, Castletownbere, Clonakilty, Cobh, Dunmanway, Doneraile, Fermoy, Kanturk, Kinsale, Macroom, Mallow, Midleton, Millstreet, Mitchelstown, Newmarket, Oileann Cleire, Passage West, Rathluirc, Rosscarbery, Schull, Skerkin Island, Skibbereen, Youghal.

Derry: Christ Church School, Windsor Terrace, Londonderry BT48 7HQ.
   Bellaghy, Coleraine, Draperstown, Dungiven, Garvagh, Kilrea, Limavady, Maghera, Magherafelt, Portstewart.

Donegal: The Courthouse, Lifford.
   Ardara, Ballybofey, Ballyshannon, Buncrana, Bundoran, Carndonagh, Carrick, Clonmany, Donegal Town, Dungloe, Glenties, Killybegs, Letterkenny, Milford, Moville, Pettigo, Raphoe, Ramelton.

Down: Windmill Hill, Ballynahinch, BT24 8DH.
   Ballynahinch, Banbridge, Bangor, Belvoir Park, Braniel, Carryduff, Castlewellan, Comber, Cregagh, Donaghadee, Downpatrick, Dromore, Dundonald, Gilford, Gilnahirk, Holywood, Kilkeel, Killyleagh, Newry, Newcastle, Newtownards, Portaferry, Rathfriland, Saintfield, Tullycarnet, Warrenpoint.

Fermanagh: Darling Street, Enniskillen.
   Enniskillen, Fermanagh, Irvinestown, Lisnaskea.

Galway: The Courthouse, Galway.
   Ahascragh, Athenry, Ballinasloe, Ballygar, Clifden, Craughwell, Creggs, Dunmore, Eyrecourt, Glenamaddy, Gort, Headford, Kilconnell, Killimore, Kilronan, Kinvara, Loughrea, Moylough, Portumna, Roundstone, Spiddal, Tuam, Williamstown, Woodford.

Kerry: Moyderwell, Tralee.
   Caherciveen, Castleisland, Dingle, Kenmare, Killarney, Killorglin, Listowel, Tralee.

Kildare: Athgarvan Road, Newbridge.
   Athy, Ballintore, Ballymore-Eustace, Castledermot, Celbridge, Clane, Coill Dubh, Curragh, Droichead Nua, Kilcock, Kilcullen, Kildare, Leixlip, Maynooth, Monasterevin, Naas, Rathangan.

Kilkenny: John Street, Kilkenny.
   Callan, Kilkenny City, Loughboy, Thomastown.

Laois: Church Street, Portlaoise.
  Abbeyleix, Mountmellick, Mountrath, Portarlington, Rathdowney, Stradbally.
Leitrim: The Courthouse, Ballinamore.
  Carrick-on-Shannon, Carrigallen, Dromahair, Drumshanbo, Kiltyclogher, Kinlough, Manorhamilton, Mohill.
Limerick: 58 O'Connell Street, Limerick.
  Abbeyfeale, Adare, Askeaton, Athea, Ballingarry, Ballylanders, Bruff, Caherconlish, Cappamore, Croom, Doon, Dorradoyle Shopping Centre, Drumcollogher, Foynes, Galbally, Glin, Hospital, Kilfinane, Kilmallock, Newcastlewest, Pallaskenry, Rathkeale, Shanagolden.
Longford: Dublin Road, Mullingar, Co. Westmeath.
  Ballymahon, Edgeworthstown, Granard, Lanesboro, Longford.
Louth: Chapel Street, Dundalk.
  Ardee, Drogheda, Dundalk.
Mayo: Mountain View, Castlebar.
  Ballina, Ballinrobe, Ballyhaunis, Castlebar, Claremorris, Crossmolina, Kiltimagh, Louisburgh, Westport.
Meath: Railway Street, Navan.
  Ashbourne, Athboy, Duleek, Dunboyne, Dunshaughlin, Kells, Kilmessan, Laytown, Navan, Oldcastle, Slane, Trim.
Monaghan: The Diamond, Clones.
  Carrickmacross, Castleblaney, Clones, Monaghan Town.
Offaly: Tullamore.
  Banagher, Birr, Clara, Daingean, Edenderry, Ferbane, Kilcormac, Shinrone, Tullamore.
Roscommon: Abbey Street.
  Ballaghaderreen, Ballyforan, Boyle, Castlerea, Elphin, Roscommon, Strokestown.
Sligo: Stephen Street, Sligo.
  Ballymote, Enniscrone, Sligo, Tubbercurry.
Tipperary: Castle Avenue, Thurles.
  Borrisokane, Borrisoleigh, Cahir, Carrick-on-Suir, Cashel, Clogheen, Clonmel, Cloghjordan, Fethard, Killenaule, Mullinahone, Nenagh, Newport, Roscrea, Templemore, Thurles, Tipperary.
Tyrone: Dublin Road, Omagh BT78 1HG.
  Castlederg, Coalisland, Cookstown, Dungannon, Fintona, Fivemiletown, Newtownstewart, Omagh, Sion Mills, Strabane.
Waterford: Lismore.
  Ballyduff Upper, Cappoquin, Dungarvan, Kilmacthomas, Lismore, Portlaw, Stradbally, Tallow, Tramore.
Westmeath: Dublin Road, Mullingar.
  Athlone, Castlepollard, Delvin, Kilbeggan, Moate, Mullingar.
Wexford: County Hall, Spawell Road, Wexford.
  Bunclody, Enniscorthy, Gorey, New Ross, Wexford.
Wicklow: Greystones.
  Arklow, Avoca, Baltinglass, Blessington, Carnew, Davidstown, Dunlavin, Enniskerry, Greystones, Knockananna, Newtown, Rathdrum, Roundwood, Shillelagh, Tinahely, Valleymount, Wicklow.

The Ancestor Trail in Ireland

County Newspapers and Towns where Published

Antrim: *Ballymena Observer,* Ballymena.
Armagh: *Armagh Guardian,* Armagh.
Carlow: *Nationalist and Leinster Times,* Carlow
Cavan: *Anglo Celt,* Cavan.
Clare: *Clare Champion,* Clare.
Cork: *Southern Star,* Skibbereen.
Derry: *Derry Journal,* Derry.
Donegal: *Donegal Democrat,* Ballyshannon.
Down: *Mourne Observer and Dromore Weekly Times,* Newcastle.
Dublin: *Evening Herald,* Dublin.
Evening Press, Dublin.
Fermanagh: *Impartial Reporter & Farmers' Journal,* Enniskillen.
Galway: *Connacht Tribune,* Galway.
Kerry: *Kerryman/Corkman,* Tralee.
Kildare: *Leinster Leader,* Naas.
Kilkenny: *Kilkenny People,* Kilkenny.
Leitrim: *Leitrim Observer,* Carrick-on-Shannon.
Laois: *Leinster Observer,* Portlaoise.
Limerick: *Limerick Leader,* Limerick.
Longford: *Longford Leader,* Longford.
Louth: *Argus,* Dundalk.
Mayo: *Connaught Telegraph,* Castlebar.
Meath: *Meath Chronicle,* Navan.
Monaghan: *Northern Standard,* Monaghan.
Offaly: *Midland Tribune,* Birr.
Roscommon: *Roscommon Champion,* Roscommon.
Sligo: *Sligo Champion,* Sligo.
Tipperary: *Tipperary Star,* Thurles.
Tyrone: *The Democrat,* Tyrone.
Waterford: *Munster Express,* Waterford.
Westmeath: *Westmeath Examiner,* Mullingar.
Wexford: *New Ross Standard,* Wexford.
Wicklow: *Wicklow People,* Wicklow.

Latin forms of Christian Names found in Baptismal Registers, with English equivalents

Latin	English
Andreas	Andrew.
Brianus	Brian, Bryan.
Brigida	Brigid, Bride, Breeda, Bridget.
Catherina	Catherine.
Demetrius	Dermod, Dermot, Darby, Jeremiah, Jerry, Jerome.
Donnchadus	Donogh, Donough, Donaghy.
Eadmundus	Eamon, Edmund, Edmond, Edward.
Giraldus	Garrett, Gerald, Gerard.
Helena	Eileen, Eveleen, Aileen, Ellen, Helen, Eily, Nellie, Lena.
Honoria	Honor, Honora, Honoria, Nora, Norah, Hannah.
Jacobus	James, Sheamus.
Joanna	Joan, Hannah, Julia, July, Judith, Judy, Susan, Nonie.
Joannes	Eoin, John, Sean.
Josephus	Joseph.
Margarita	Margaret, Maggie, Madge.
Maria	Mary.
Martinus	Martin.
Patricius	Patrick.
Thaddaeus	Teige, Teague, Thady, Thade, Timothy, Tim.

A Companion Guide

Area Registries of Births, Marriages and Deaths

Carlow	St. Dympna's Hospital, Carlow.
Cavan	The Courthouse, Cavan.
Clare	The Courthouse, Ennis.
Cork (North)	County Offices, Mallow.
Cork (South)	18, Liberty Street, Cork.
Cork (West)	The Courthouse, Skibbereen.
Donegal (North)	Supt. Regr's Office, Letterkenny.
Donegal (South)	Stranorlar, Co. Donegal.
Dublin	8-11 Lombard Street East, Dublin 2
Galway	County Buildings, Galway.
Kerry	Central Register Office, Killarney.
Kildare	Basin Street, Naas.
Kilkenny	John's Green, Kilkenny.
Laois	The Courthouse, Portlaoise.
Leitrim	Courthouse, Carrick-on-Shannon.
Limerick (City)	St. Camillus's Hospital, Limerick.
Limerick (County)	Newcastle West.
Longford	Co. Clinic, Longford.
Louth	Courthouse, Dundalk.
Mayo	Town Hall, Castlebar.
Meath	The Courthouse, Trim.
Monaghan	Rooskey, Monaghan.
Offaly	The Health Centre, Tullamore.
Roscommon	The Courthouse, Roscommon.
Sligo	Markievicz House, Sligo
Tipperary (North)	Hospital of the Assumption, Thurles.
Tipperary (South)	Supt. Regr's Office, Clonmel.
Waterford (City)	St. Patrick's Hospital, Waterford.
Waterford (County)	Árus Brugha, Dungarvan.
Wexford	Co. Clinic, Grogan's Road, Wexford.
Wicklow	Kilmantin Hill, Wicklow.

31

USEFUL BOOKS

Irish Christian Names
> *Irish Names for Children:* G. Slevin, Dublin, 1974.
> *Irish Christian Names:* Ronan Coghlan, London, 1979.
> *Gaelic Personal Names:* Donnchadh Ó Corráin and Fidelma Maguire, Dublin 1981.

Irish Surnames
> *Varieties and Synonyms of Surnames and Christian Names in Ireland:* Robert E. Matheson, Dublin, 1890.
> *Surnames in Ireland:* Robert E. Matheson, Dublin, 1984.
> *Irish Names and Surnames:* Rev. Patrick Woulfe, Dublin, 1923.
> *The Surnames of Ireland:* Edward MacLysaght, Dublin, 1985.
> *Irish Families, Their Names, Arms and Origins:* Edward MacLysaght, Dublin, 1985.

Distribution of Surnames in Ireland
> County Indexes: List of surnames in each county of all persons given in the General Valuation and Tithe Books, 1820-1865, National Library of Ireland, 1963.

Irish Folklore
> *The Year in Ireland:* Kevin Danaher, Cork, 1972.
> *Ulster Folklore:* Jeanne Cooper Foster, Belfast, 1951.

Irish Place-names
> *Irish Names of Places:* P.W. Joyce, 1 & 2, Dublin, 1869, 1875.
> *Alphabetical Index to the Townlands and Towns of Ireland:* H.M.S.O., Dublin, 1861.
> *Irish Local Names Explained:* P.W. Joyce, Dublin, 1884.
> 'Name Books': John O'Donovan, 1830-1840. (Contains detailed account of place-names parish by parish in each county).
> *A Topographical Dictionary of Ireland:* Samuel Lewis, 1837.
> *The Shell Guide to Ireland:* Lord Killanin & Michael Duignan, 1967.
> *Kelly's Directory of Ireland:* Very Extensive, 1905.

Lists of Clergy
> Roman Catholic: *Irish Catholic Directory.*
> Church of Ireland: (Protestant) *Church of Ireland Directory.*

Guide Books on Ancestry Tracing
> *Handbook on Irish Genealogy:* Heraldic Artists, Dublin, 1984.
> *Irish Genealogy: A Record Finder:* Heraldic Artists, Dublin, 1981.

Irish History
> *A Little History of Ireland:* Seamus MacCall, Dublin, 1980.
> *The Course of Irish History:* T.W Moody & F.X. Martin, Cork, 1984.